GRADE SIX

Electric Guitar Playing

compiled by

Tony Skinner

on behalf of

RGT®

Registry of Guitar Tutors

A CIP record for this publication is available from the British Library

ISBN 1-898466-56-4

© 2001 & 2005 The Registry of Guitar Tutors
The Guitarograph is a trade mark of The Registry of Guitar Tutors

Published in Great Britain by

Registry Mews, 11 to 13 Wilton Road, Bexhill, Sussex, TN40 1HY

Music and text typesetting by

54 Lincolns Mead, Lingfield, Surrey RH7 6TA

Printed and bound in Great Britain

Contents

Introduction

This handbook is primarily intended to give advice and information to candidates considering taking the Grade Six examination in electric guitar playing, although undoubtedly it will be found that the information contained within will be helpful to all guitarists whether intending to take the examination or not.

GUITAROGRAPH

In order that scales, arpeggios and chords can be illustrated as clearly as possible, and made available for all to understand regardless of experience, notation and fingering are displayed via the use of the *guitarograph*.

The *guitarograph* uses a combination of tablature, traditional notation and fingerboard diagram – thereby ensuring clarity and leaving no doubt as to what is required. In the example shown above, all three notations refer to the same note, i.e. A on the 2nd fret of the 3rd (G) string, fretted with the 2nd finger. Each of the notation methods used in the *guitarograph* is explained below:

Tablature

The tablature is shown on the left of the guitarograph, with horizontal lines representing the strings (with the high E string being string 1), and the numbers on the string lines referring to the frets. A '0' on a line would mean play that string *open* (unfretted).

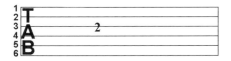   This means play at the second fret on the third string.

Musical notation

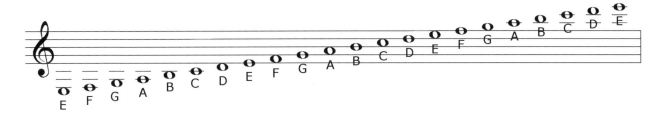

Notation on the treble clef is shown in the centre of the guitarograph.

A sharp (♯) before a note would raise its pitch by a semitone i.e. one fret higher, whilst a flat (♭) before a note would lower the pitch by a semitone, i.e. one fret lower. A natural sign (♮) before a note cancels a sharp or flat sign. A double sharp sign (𝄪) raises a note by a whole tone. A double flat sign (♭♭) lowers a note by a whole tone.

Fingerboard diagram

The fingerboard diagram is shown on the right of the guitarograph with horizontal lines representing the strings. Vertical lines represent the frets, with fret numbers shown in Roman numerals. The numbers on the horizontal lines show the recommended fingering. Fingerings have been chosen which are likely to be the most effective for the widest range of players at this level, however there are a variety of alternative fingerings and fingerboard positions that could be used and you can use any other systematic fingerings that produce a good musical result.

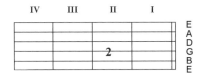

This means play with the second finger at the second fret on the G string.

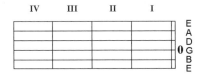

This means play the G string *open*, i.e. without fretting it.

Interval spellings

Above each guitarograph is an interval spelling. This lists the letter names of the notes within the scale, arpeggio or chord, together with their interval numbers. The interval numbers shown are based on their comparison to the major scale with the same starting pitch. The scale, arpeggio and chord spellings will help you identify the differences in construction between the various scales and chords, and will help you learn the names of the notes that you are playing.

For example:

A major scale									A natural minor scale							
A	B	C♯	D	E	F♯	G♯	A		A	B	C	D	E	F	G	A
1	2	3	4	5	6	7	8		1	2	♭3	4	5	♭6	♭7	8

Scales and arpeggios

At this grade candidates should be able to play the following scales in *any* key:

- 1 octave natural minor and major scales, in 5 different fingerboard positions

- 2 octave Dorian and Mixolydian modal scales

- 2 octave chromatic scale

- 1 octave major scale and pentatonic minor scale in 8ths

- 1 octave major scale in 3rds

In addition, candidates should be able to play, in 2 different fingerboard positions, the following 1 octave arpeggios starting from *any* note:

- augmented 5th
- diminished 7th
- minor 9th

- dominant 9th
- major 9th

Candidates should also have a practical knowledge of the requirements from the previous grade.

This chapter contains examples of the Grade Six scales and arpeggios. All these use transpositional finger patterns, so each shape can be moved up or down the fingerboard to a new pitch without the need for a change of fingering.

The table below can be used to learn the starting fret for different pitches. For example, to play the B chromatic scale (rather than A as shown on page 10): notice that the guitarograph is illustrated with its keynote on the 6th string; find the note B on the 6th string (at the 7th fret); start the same pattern from the 7th fret, rather than from the 5th.

scales or arpeggios with keynote on the:	... Fret Number ...											
	1 or 13	2 or 14	3 or 15	4	5	6	7	8	9	10	11	12
3rd string	G#/Ab	A	A#/Bb	B	C	C#/Db	D	D#/Eb	E	F	F#/Gb	G
4th string	D#/Eb	E	F	F#/Gb	G	G#/Ab	A	A#/Bb	B	C	C#/Db	D
5th string	A#/Bb	B	C	C#/Db	D	D#/Eb	E	F	F#/Gb	G	G#/Ab	A
6th string	F	F#/Gb	G	G#/Ab	A	A#/Bb	B	C	C#/Db	D	D#/Eb	E

Scales

A NATURAL MINOR SCALE – 1 OCTAVE (five different fingerboard positions)

A	B	C	D	E	F	G	A
1	2	♭3	4	5	♭6	♭7	8

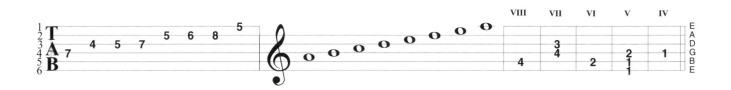

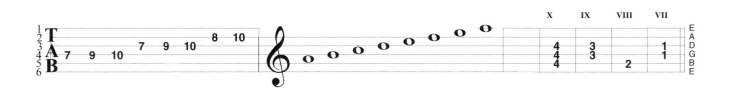

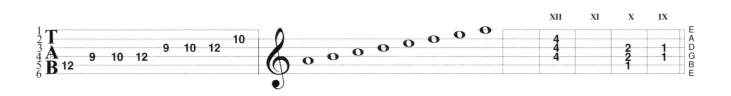

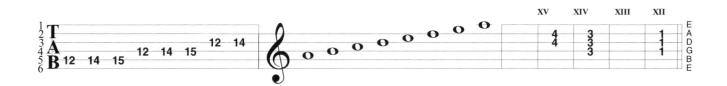

8

A MAJOR SCALE – 1 OCTAVE (five different fingerboard positions)

A	B	C♯	D	E	F♯	G♯	A
1	2	3	4	5	6	7	8

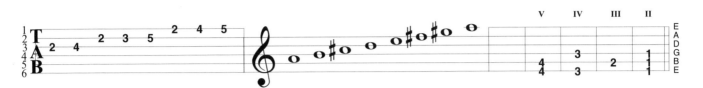

A DORIAN MODAL SCALE – 2 OCTAVES

This can also be referred to as the Dorian (or 2nd) mode of the key of G major

A	B	C	D	E	F♯	G	A
1	2	♭3	4	5	6	♭7	8

9

A MIXOLYDIAN MODAL SCALE – 2 OCTAVES
This can also be referred to as the Mixolydian (or 5th) mode of the key of D major

A	B	C♯	D	E	F♯	G	A
1	2	3	4	5	6	♭7	8

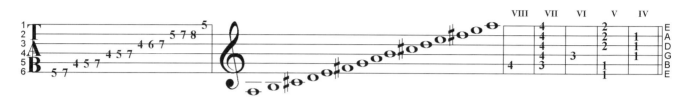

A CHROMATIC SCALE – 2 OCTAVES

A	B♭	B	C	C♯	D	D♯	E	F	F♯	G	G♯	A
1	♭2	2	♭3	3	4	♯4	5	♭6	6	♭7	7	8

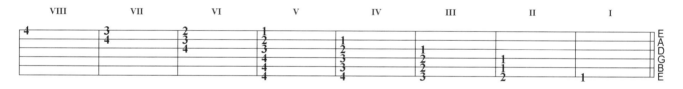

A MAJOR SCALE IN 8THS – 1 OCTAVE

A	B	C♯	D	E	F♯	G♯	A
1	2	3	4	5	6	7	8

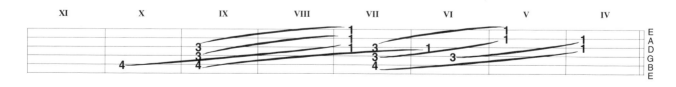

A PENTATONIC MINOR SCALE IN 8THS – 1 OCTAVE

A	C	D	E	G	A
1	♭3	4	5	♭7	8

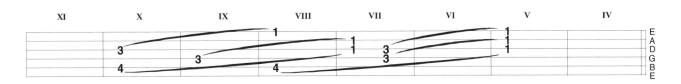

A MAJOR SCALE IN 3RDS – 1 OCTAVE

1	2	3	4	5	6	7	8
A	B	C♯	D	E	F♯	G♯	A
C♯	D	E	F♯	G♯	A	B	C♯

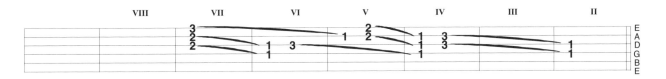

Arpeggios

C AUGMENTED 5TH ARPEGGIO – 1 OCTAVE (Root on the E string)

C	E	G♯	C
1	3	♯5	8

C AUGMENTED 5TH ARPEGGIO – 1 OCTAVE (Root on the A string)

C	E	G♯	C
1	3	♯5	8

11

C DIMINISHED 7TH ARPEGGIO – 1 OCTAVE (Root on the E string)

C Eb Gb Bbb C
1 b3 b5 bb7 8

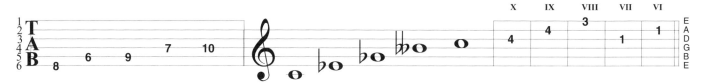

C DIMINISHED 7TH ARPEGGIO – 1 OCTAVE (Root on the A string)

C Eb Gb Bbb C
1 b3 b5 bb7 8

C MINOR 9TH ARPEGGIO – 1 OCTAVE (Root on the E string)

C Eb G Bb D
1 b3 5 b7 9

C MINOR 9TH ARPEGGIO – 1 OCTAVE (Root on the A string)

C Eb G Bb D
1 b3 5 b7 9

C DOMINANT 9TH ARPEGGIO – 1 OCTAVE (Root on the E string)

C E G Bb D
1 3 5 b7 9

C DOMINANT 9TH ARPEGGIO – 1 OCTAVE (Root on the A string)

C MAJOR 9TH ARPEGGIO – 1 OCTAVE (Root on the E string)

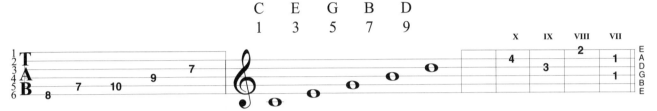

C MAJOR 9TH ARPEGGIO – 1 OCTAVE (Root on the A string)

INFORMATION AND ADVICE

A maximum of 10 marks may be awarded in this section of the examination. The examiner may request you to play, from memory, any of the required scales and arpeggios. Each should be played once only, ascending and descending (i.e. from the lowest note to the highest and back again) without a pause and without repeating the top note. Candidates will not be asked to play in fingerboard positions that are inaccessible for their particular instrument. Candidates should be able to demonstrate any scale or arpeggio promptly, without hesitation.

When the examiner requests scales or arpeggios in more than one fingerboard position, these do not have to be the positions illustrated in this book: other systematic and effective fingerings may be acceptable, providing that different fingerboard positions of the same scale or arpeggio are played in the same octave, wherever possible.

As a guideline, non-harmonised scales should be played at a tempo of approximately 144 beats per minute (two notes per beat), with arpeggios a little slower at approximately 112 bpm, and harmonised scales at approximately 52 bpm. Choose a tempo at which you feel confident and comfortable and try to maintain this evenly throughout: evenness and clarity are more important than speed for its own sake.

Chords

At this grade candidates should be able to play the following chords at any pitch, in two different fingerboard positions:

- major 9th
- minor 9th
- dominant 9th

- diminished 7th
- augmented 5th

In addition, candidates should be familiar with the chords set for the previous grade.

The chords below are illustrated with a root note of C, however, because they utilise transpositional shapes they can be moved up or down the fingerboard to any pitch without the need to change fingering.

This table lists the fret position needed to produce chords at different pitches.

Root note on fret number:	1	2	3	4	5	6	7	8	9	10	11	12
Chords with root on E string:	F	F♯/G♭	G	G♯/A♭	A	A♯/B♭	B	C	C♯/D♭	D	D♯/E♭	E
Chords with root on A string:	A♯/B♭	B	C	C♯/D♭	D	D♯/E♭	E	F	F♯/G♭	G	G♯/A♭	A

C major 9th (Cmaj9 – root on E string)

C   E   G   B   D

1   3   5   7   9

C major 9th (Cmaj9 – root on A string)

C   E   G   B   D

1   3   5   7   9

C minor 9th (Cm9 – root on E string)

C	E♭	G	B♭	D
1	♭3	5	♭7	9

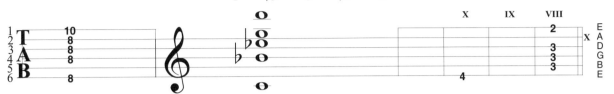

C minor 9th (Cm9 – root on A string)

C	E♭	G	B♭	D
1	♭3	5	♭7	9

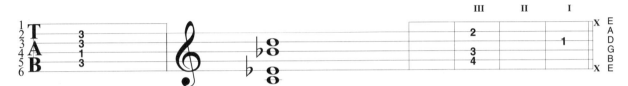

C dominant 9th (C9 – root on E string)

C	E	G	B♭	D
1	3	5	♭7	9

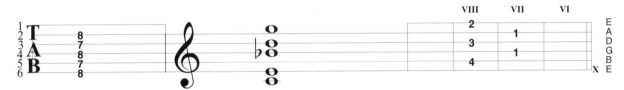

C dominant 9th (C9 – root on A string)

C	E	G	B♭	D
1	3	5	♭7	9

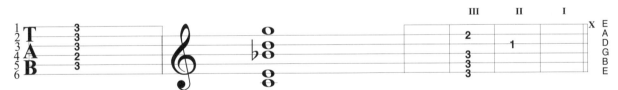

C diminished 7th (C° – root on E string)

C	E♭	G♭	B♭♭
1	♭3	♭5	♭♭7

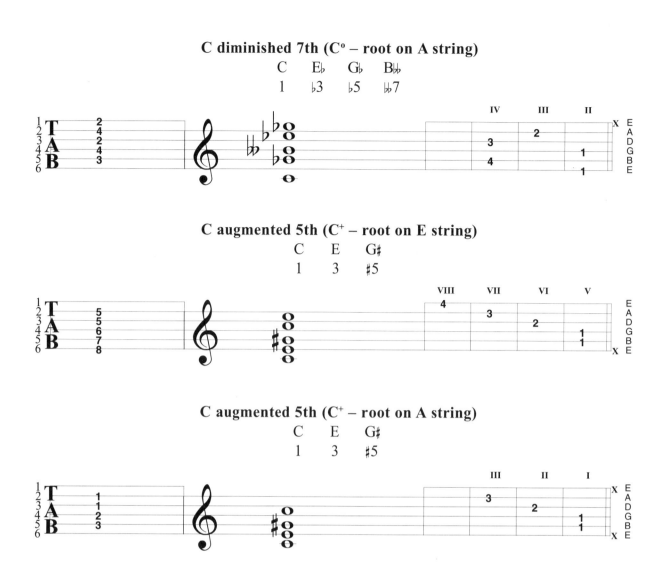

INFORMATION AND ADVICE

A maximum of 8 marks may be awarded in this section of the examination. The examiner may request you to play, from memory, any of the required chords in two different fingerboard positions. Each chord shape should be played once only, using a single downstroke. You should be able to demonstrate any chord promptly, without hesitation.

In the fingerboard diagrams, strings which should not be sounded are marked by an 'x'. If these are lower in pitch than the root, then care should be taken not to strike these strings, or the strings should be muted by touching them lightly with the pad of the thumb or with the tip of the finger which is fretting the adjacent higher pitched string. If the unwanted strings fall elsewhere within the chord, the finger fretting the adjacent lower pitched string will need to be positioned so as to touch and mute the unwanted string. To ensure clarity and accuracy, make sure that your fingers are carefully and correctly positioned before playing the chord.

Rhythm playing

In this section of the examination, the candidate will be shown a chord chart and will be allowed a short time (of about 30 seconds) to study it before being asked to play it. The chord chart will contain only chords listed in Section 2 of this book, together with those required for previous grades.

After playing the first chord chart candidates may, at the examiner's discretion, be given an additional chart to play; this will be of similar difficulty to the first.

Some examples of the *type* of chart that may be presented at this grade are given below. The tempo markings are intended only as broad guidelines.

(i) Bright and rhythmical

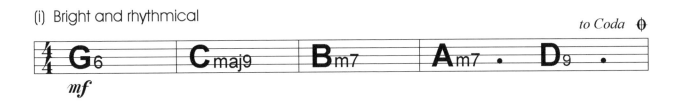

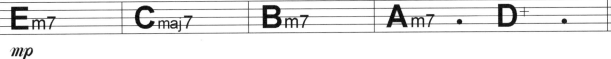

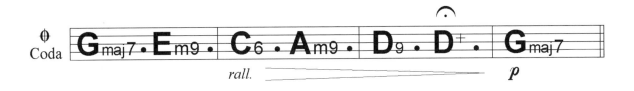

(ii) Fairly slow

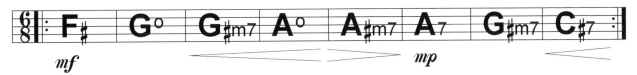

(iii) Slowly with expression

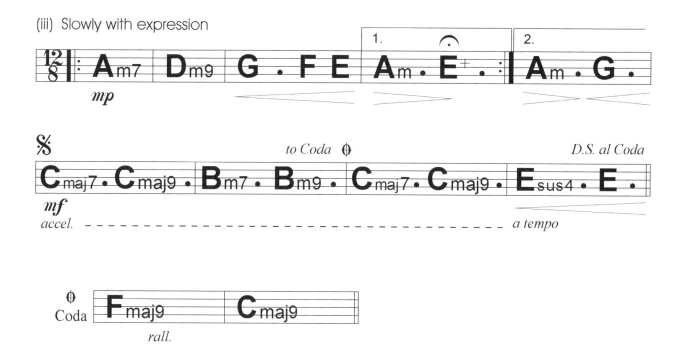

In practice, musicians may write out chord charts not only on staves (as shown above) but sometimes chords are written above staves instead, or quite commonly just with bar lines (as in the example below). In the examination, to achieve maximum visual clarity, all chord charts will be presented in the style shown below.

(iv) Not too slow

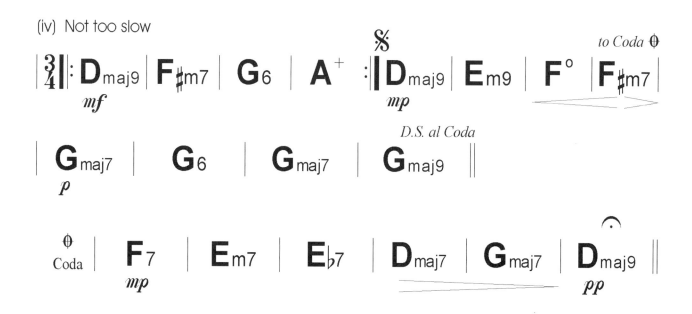

Split bars

When two (or more) chords appear in a single bar this is known as a split bar. Dots (or diagonal lines) after chords can be used to indicate the division of the bar: the chord symbol representing one beat and each dot representing another beat. If no dots are present it can be assumed that the bar is divided evenly between the chords.

INFORMATION AND ADVICE

A maximum of 25 marks may be awarded in this section of the examination. The examiner will award marks primarily for accuracy (including attention to time signature, repeat and interpretaion marks), clarity, fluency, inventiveness and the overall musicality of the performance.

At this grade the time signature is limited to either $\frac{3}{4}$, $\frac{4}{4}$, $\frac{6}{8}$ or $\frac{12}{8}$ time. Whilst the time signature should be evident by generally maintaining a regular pulse and even tempo, candidates are expected to be imaginative in their rhythm playing.

The musical style that is used is left to the discretion of the candidate, and fingerpicking can be used, rather than strumming, if preferred by the candidate.

Chords should ring clear, i.e. free of fret-buzz or the unintended muting of notes with the fretting-hand fingers. Chord changes should be as smooth and fluid as possible and lack any sense of hesitation. Care should be taken, when choosing which chord shape to use, that large fingerboard jumps between chords are avoided whenever possible.

During the time given to look over the chord chart, candidates should try to discover the overall structure of the progression, paying attention to time signature, repeat signs, dynamics and other indications. In particular, candidates should be able to interpret the following indications which may be marked on the chord chart:

Repeat marks

Passages to be repeated are indicated by two vertical dots at the start and end of the section to be repeated. For example:

should be played as:

There are other signs that indicate which sections are to be repeated:

D.C. (Da Capo – from the head) means play again from the beginning.

D.S. (Dal Segno – from the sign) means play from the sign (%).

Al Coda (to the tail) means play the end section. This is marked with a coda sign (ϕ).

Example (i):

should be played as:

Example (ii):

should be played as:

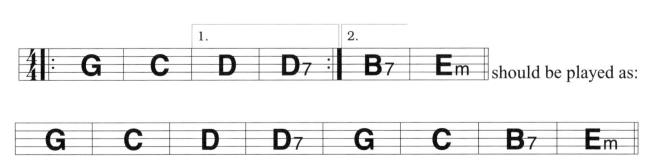

1st and 2nd time endings

Bars marked ⌐1.⌐ are included in the first playing but omitted on the repeat playing and replaced with the bars marked ⌐2.⌐ For example :

should be played as:

Dynamic markings

These are indications to show the range of, and changes in, volume.

ppp	*pp*	*p*	*mp*	*mf*	*f*	*ff*	*fff*
⇕		⇕		⇕			⇕
play as softly as possible		play softly		moderately loud			play as strongly as possible

< – become louder   > – become softer

Tempo changes

Accel. (accelerando) – Gradually faster

Rall. (rallentando) – Gradually slower

A tempo (in time) – Resume normal speed after a deviation

⌢ (pause) – Hold longer than the written value

DAMPING TECHNIQUES

When musically appropriate, candidates should display some level of skill in string damping during the performance.

Fretting-hand damping (choking)

This is achieved by slightly relaxing the pressure on the strings you are fretting: the fingers are still touching the strings, but are not pressing them all the way down to the fretboard. This technique can be used after a chord has been strummed to achieve a staccato effect or chord 'chop'. The technique can also be used to bring out accents, by damping the fretting hand continuously whilst the strumming hand plays a rhythm – the fretting hand only pressing the chord intermittently, so that it sounds only on the beats to be accented.

Strumming-hand damping

By resting the side of the strumming hand lightly on the strings, close to the saddle, a choked or muted sound can be achieved by deadening the sustain of the chords. This technique can be used after a chord has been strummed to achieve a staccato effect. The technique can also be used to bring out accents in a rhythm, by maintaining the muting effect throughout and releasing only intermittently on the beats to be accented.

Lead playing

In this section of the examination, the candidate will be shown a chord progression containing chords from Section 2 of this book, as well as chords listed in previous grades. The examiner will then play this progression (either live or recorded) and the candidate should improvise over this using appropriate scales and arpeggios selected from Section 1 of this book.

Some examples of the *type* of chord chart that will be presented at this grade are shown below. The scale and arpeggio suggestions are given for guidance in this book, but will NOT appear in the examination.

(i) The A major scale could be used as the basis for improvisation, but with arpeggios used over the diminished and augmented chords, and perhaps over the two bars of Dmaj9.

(ii) The A Dorian modal scale could be used as the basis for improvisation, with chord tones from arpeggios emphasized in places (particularly when a chord lasts for two bars).

(iii) B natural minor scale could be used as the basis for improvisation, with an arpeggio used over the F♯7 chord (particularly where it lasts for two bars).

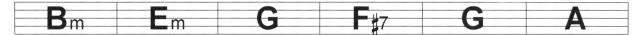

(iv) C natural minor scale could be used as the basis for improvisation, but with an arpeggio used over the G9 chord.

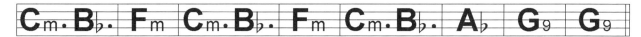

INFORMATION AND ADVICE

The progression will be played a total of four times; during the first playing the candidate should not play, but rather listen and digest the progression, before improvising over the next three cycles. After the final playing the progression will end on the key chord. The time signature will be limited to those set in Section Three.

To ensure accuracy it is essential that the candidate selects the most appropriate scales and arpeggios with which to improvise. The examiner will NOT advise on this.

At the examiner's discretion an additional progression may be selected for the candidate to improvise over. This may be in a different key from the first progression.

Gaining marks

A maximum of 25 marks may be awarded in this section of the examination. The examiner will award marks for:

- accuracy
- fluency
- a confident and assured performance
- phrasing and melodic shaping
- stylistic interpretation
- inventiveness and creativity
- clarity and tone production
- the application of specialist techniques

Endeavour to make your improvisation melodically and rhythmically inventive and imaginative, rather than sounding scale-like. The use of movement and interplay between different fingerboard positions will help in this objective.

The style of lead playing should enhance and empathise with the chordal accompaniment, which may be from a range of popular music styles such as rock, jazz, pop, soul, ballad, blues, funk, etc. Try to create interesting melodic and rhythmic phrases within your improvisation and avoid inappropriate use of continuous scalic playing. Playing should be fluent, but without the need for speed for its own sake; more important is the overall musical effect that is achieved.

At this grade, candidates' lead playing might be enhanced by the application of arpeggios during the performance, when musically appropriate. In addition, candidates might find that at least some basic use of chromaticism, i.e. the occasional interjection of passing notes, could add to the general musical effect.

SPECIALIST TECHNIQUES

At this grade, *when musically appropriate*, candidates ideally should be able to demonstrate skill in the use of some of the following techniques during their improvisation:

- String bending: candidates should be adept in executing both half-tone and whole-tone bends.

- Vibrato: candidates should have good control over a range of vibrato techniques, including wrist and finger generated vibrato.

- Slurs: candidates should be fluent in the use of hammer-ons, pull-offs and trills.

- Double stops: candidates should have some basic skill in playing in 3rds, 5ths or octaves.

- Pick control: candidates should use a range of attack in striking the strings, and should be able to use this ability to vary volume and tone whilst playing.

Spoken tests

A maximum of 12 marks may be awarded in this section of the examination.

FINGERBOARD KNOWLEDGE

At this grade candidates will be expected to confidently and promptly name any note on any string.

Candidates may also be asked to name the notes that relate to the diatonic intervals of *any* major scale, up to an including a major 9th. For example, candidates may be asked to identify the note that forms a major 9th interval above C (i.e. D). The diagram below, shows the notes and diatonic intervals in the C major scale; the fingerings are transpositional to other keys.

During this section of the examination candidates will *not* be allowed to play the guitar to 'work-out' answers to this test.

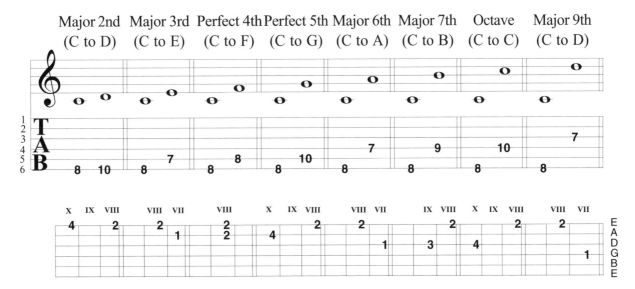

Enharmonic spelling

C major contains no sharps or flats, but in other major keys candidates will need to be careful to give the notes the correct 'enharmonic spelling'. For example, the major 7th interval in G major is F♯, not G♭. (Although these two notes will sound the same, G major is a 'sharp key' and so the sharp equivalent is used when describing this note.)

Sharp keys: G D A E B F♯. Use the ♯ equivalent for notes from these major scales; no flat notes should be used.
Flat keys: F B♭ E♭ A♭ D♭ G♭. Use the ♭ equivalent for notes from these major scales; no sharp notes should be used.

APPLICATION OF SCALES, ARPEGGIOS AND CHORDS

Candidates may be asked questions about the scales and arpeggios listed in Section One of this book, in particular, being asked to explain their function and identify groups of chords with which each scale could be used. For example, A natural minor scale would fit over a chord sequence consisting of A minor and D minor, whereas the A Dorian modal scale would fit better over a chord sequence of A minor and D *major*. A typical question might be: "Give an example of a scale which could be used to improvise over a chord sequence consisting of C9 and B♭maj7". Acceptable answers would be C Mixolydian modal scale, or the Mixolydian mode of F major, or even F major scale.

It is essential that candidates are aware of which chords occur in each key, so that the correct analysis of a chord progression can be made.

It is highly recommended that candidates who are unsure in this area study the London College of Music Exams 'Popular Music Theory' handbooks as an ideal supplement to this examination.

Candidates should also be able to explain the appropriate use of extended chords, such as 9th chords. For example:

- a minor 9th chord can be used to replace and extend a minor or minor 7th chord;

- a dominant 9th chord can be used to replace and extend a dominant 7th chord (normally built on the 5th degree of the scale);

- a major 9th chord can be used to replace and extend a major or major 7th chord (normally built on the 1st or 4th degree of the major scale).

TONE PRODUCTION

Candidates should be aware of the optimum position of the fretting-hand fingers, in regard to achieving clarity and avoiding fret buzz. The most important factor being to press very close to the fretwire, and (except when holding a barre with the first finger) to use the tips rather than the pads of the fingers.

Candidates should have knowledge of the ways in which the tone can be varied on their own instrument. This should include:

(i)   A practical understanding of the use of tone controls and pick-up selectors (where appropriate).

(ii) An understanding of the effect of changing the right-hand position: playing at the bridge end generates the brightest tone, whilst movement towards the fingerboard tends to mellow the tone.

(iii) Knowledge of the effect of plectrum gauge and string gauge on tone production: a thicker plectrum and/or heavier strings can produce a fuller and more rounded tone than their lighter equivalents.

(iv) Knowledge of the effect on tone production caused by the angle, pace and strength with which the plectrum strikes the strings.

KNOWLEDGE OF THE INSTRUMENT

Candidates should have a thorough understanding of the mechanism and anatomy of their guitar, including such terms as:

(i) *Action* – the distance between the strings and the frets, which determines the ease of fretting notes. Candidates should be aware of how to adjust the action on their own instrument, and should be able to explain the relative advantages and disadvantages of raising or lowering the action. For example, a high action, whilst adding increased volume and a fuller tone, will require more effort in fretting notes; whereas a low action will require less finger pressure, so facilitating faster playing, but the tone and volume may be impaired and some fret buzz may occur.

(ii) *Marker dots* (fret markers) – the dots or blocks inlaid into front and/or side of the fingerboard to act as a reminder as to the position of certain frets. These normally include at least frets 3, 5, 7, 9 and 12.

(iii) *The nut* – a slotted piece of material (normally plastic or brass), situated at the headstock end of the fingerboard, in the grooves of which the strings lie.

(iv) *The saddle* – the seat upon which the strings rest at the bridge end of the guitar. It is from this point that the vibrating section of the string starts. Electric guitars tend to have an individual saddle for each string, which form part of the bridge. Candidates should be aware of how to adjust the position and height of the saddle(s) on their own instrument (if appropriate).

(v) *Machine Heads* – the turning keys, normally positioned on the guitar headstock, which when rotated increase or reduce string tension and so raise or lower the pitch of the string. Candidates should be able to explain and demonstrate at least two methods of achieving standard relative tuning, excluding using an electronic tuning aid, such as the 'fifth fret method', using harmonics or tuning to a chord.

(vi) *Strings* – candidates should be aware of how to replace a string on their own instrument. In addition, candidates should be able to explain the relative merits of different gauge strings. For example, very light strings have less tension and are easier to fret and bend, whereas heavier strings tend to hold their tuning better and produce greater volume and sustain.

Aural assessments

A maximum of 10 marks may be awarded in total during this section of the examination. The candidate will be given a selection of the following tests, which will include a rhythm test and at least two other tests. The examiner may play the tests either on guitar or keyboard.

REPETITION OF RHYTHMS

The examiner will twice play (on a single note) a four bar rhythm in either $\frac{3}{4}$, $\frac{4}{4}$ or $\frac{6}{8}$ time. This will contain no note value shorter than a sixteenth note (semiquaver). The third bar will be a repeat of the first bar, whilst the fourth bar will be a *variation* of the second bar. The candidate should reproduce the rhythm by clapping, tapping or playing. Some examples of the *type* of rhythm are given below.

REPETITION OF MELODIC PHRASES

The candidate will be asked to look away while the examiner plays a one bar phrase in either $\frac{4}{4}$ or $\frac{6}{8}$ time. This will consist of notes, within a range of one octave, from a scale listed in Section 1 of this book. The candidate will be told which scale is to be used, and the keynote will be played. The phrase, which may start from any degree of the scale, will contain no note value shorter than an eighth note (quaver).

The examiner will play the phrase twice before the candidate makes a first attempt to reproduce the phrase on the guitar. If required, the candidate can request the examiner to play the phrase one further time, prior to the candidate's second attempt. However, the candidate will then be expected to reproduce the phrase promptly, and will not be permitted any further attempts at 'working it out'. Some examples of the *type* of phrase are shown below.

The examples are taken from the following scales :

(i)

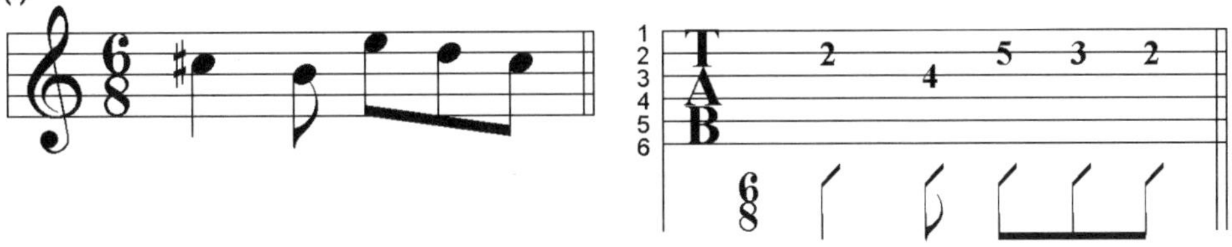

A major

(ii)

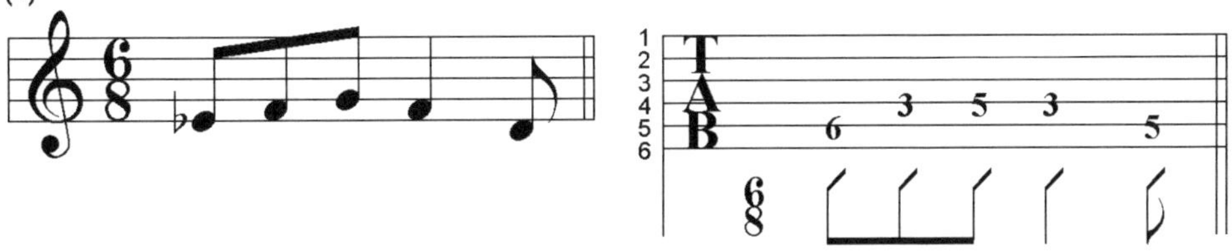

C natural minor

(iii)

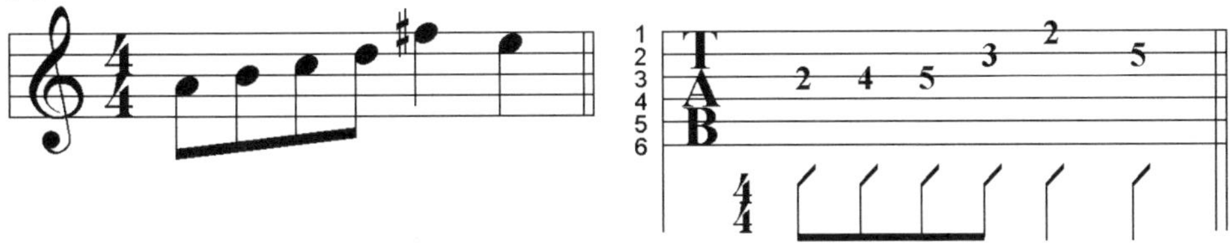

A Dorian
modal scale

(iv)

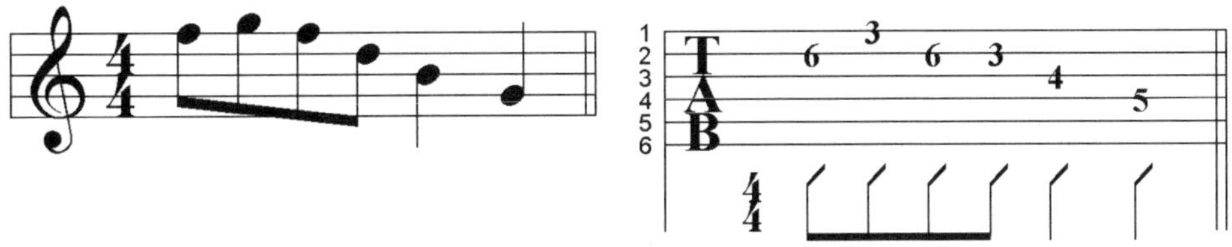

G Mixolydian
modal scale

KEEPING TIME

The examiner will twice play a four bar melody in either ¾, ⁴₄, ⁶₈ or ¹²₈ time. The melody will *not* begin on the first beat of the bar. After the first playing the candidate should identify the time signature. During the second playing the candidate should clap the main pulse, accenting the first beat of each bar. An example is given below, with the rhythmic pulse to be clapped by the candidate shown below both the notation and tablature.

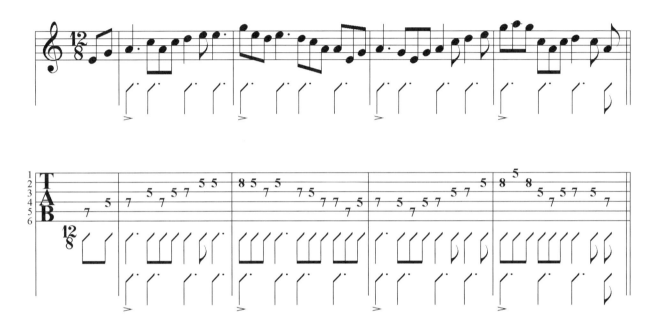

PITCH TEST

The candidate may be asked to identify any diatonic note from *any* major scale, up to a major 9th, plus the diminished and augmented 5th. Whilst the candidate looks away the examiner will state and play the keynote followed by another note. The candidate will then be asked to identify the second note either by letter name or interval number.

Here is an example of the note choices in the key of A.

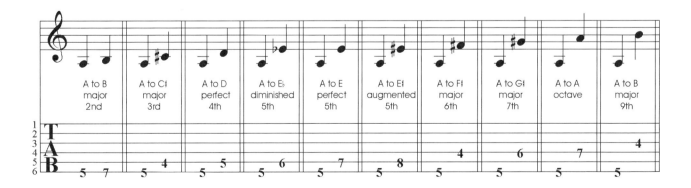

HARMONY TEST

Whilst the candidate looks away, the examiner will twice play two chords of the same nature. The candidate will then be asked to identify the *type* of chord that was played. The chord types will be selected from the following list:

- minor 7th

- dominant 7th

- major 7th

- minor 9th

- dominant 9th

- major 9th

Here are some examples:

(i)	|	A9	|	D9	||	= Dominant 9th
(ii)	|	Dm9	|	Gm9	||	= Minor 9th
(iii)	|	B♭maj7	|	E♭maj7	||	= Major 7th

Specialisms

This section of the examination provides an opportunity for candidates to choose, and display their skill and knowledge in, one of the specialist areas of guitar playing listed below. These are divided into three 'option' groups which are explained below. A maximum of 10 marks may be awarded in this section of the examination.

OPTION 1

- Slide / bottleneck playing, *or*...

- Finger-tapping, *or*...

- Fingerstyle (or flatpicking).

The music performed may be a single piece or a series of excerpts (lasting about two minutes in total), and may be an existing guitar piece or a self-composition or arrangement. The performance does not need to consist entirely of the chosen technique – providing it is the main feature of the performance.

It is preferable if the piece is played from memory, although this is not essential. *All performances must be unaccompanied.*

There are no recommended 'set pieces' as the aim is to encourage candidates to use this section of the exam to make their own musical choices and display their own musical interests and ideas. The technical level of the chosen piece (providing it is not unduly simple) is not the paramount assessment criteria, instead the examiner will be awarding marks based on the level of musicality displayed during the performance. In particular, candidates should demonstrate good control over the instrument, in a fluent performance containing expression, phrasing and dynamics. The performance should be assured, and with an appropriate sense of musical character and style.

Any candidate wishing to use an alternative tuning should be able to change to this tuning promptly and accurately, or (preferably) have another instrument ready-tuned for this purpose.

OPTION 2

- Sight reading from standard treble clef notation or from tablature.

Candidates selecting this option will be presented with a short melody to play at sight. This can be in either standard notation or tablature – at the candidate's choice. The examiner will award marks primarily for accuracy, fluency and clear phrasing.

Standard notation

- The time signature may be $\frac{3}{4}$, $\frac{4}{4}$, $\frac{6}{8}$ or $\frac{12}{8}$

- The key signature will range up to 3 sharps or 3 flats.

- The pitch will range within 3 octaves from low E.

- The rhythm may include 16th notes (semiquavers), dotted notes and ties.

An example is given below.

Moderate

Tablature

- The pitch will range within 3 octaves of the open 6th string, i.e. up to the 12th fret 1st string.

- The rhythm will be illustrated and may include 16th notes (semiquavers), dotted notes and ties, with a time signature of either $\frac{3}{4}$, $\frac{4}{4}$, $\frac{6}{8}$ or $\frac{12}{8}$

An example is given below.

$\bullet. = 60$

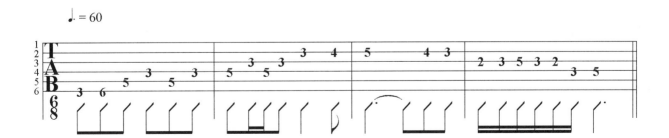

OPTION 3

- Rhythm guitar playing, *or...*

- Improvisation.

Rhythm guitar playing

The candidate will be shown a chord chart and will be allowed a short time to study it before being asked to play it. The chord chart will contain only chords listed in Section 2 of this book, together with those required for previous grades. The chord chart will be of a similar style, and level, to that used in 'Rhythm Guitar Playing' section of the exam.

Improvisation

The candidate will be shown a chord progression containing chords from Section 2 of this book, as well as chords listed in previous grades. The examiner will then play this progression (either live or recorded) and the candidate should improvise over this. The progression will be played a total of four times; during the first playing the candidate should not play, but rather listen and digest the progression, before improvising over the next three cycles. The chord chart will be of a similar style, and complexity, to that used in 'Lead Guitar Playing' section of the exam.